Written by Lisa McCourt
Illustrated by Monika Popowitz

Photography by Steve Dolce

 HOUGHTON MIFFLIN   BOSTON · MORRIS PLAINS, NJ

California   ·   Colorado   ·   Georgia   ·   Illinois   ·   New Jersey   ·   Texas

For Cheryl Nathan—L.M.

Many thanks to all my friends and family for their support
—M.P.

Raptors were fierce
hunting dinosaurs.

3

Sharp teeth lined their powerful jaws.

Three long, hooked claws grew out of each arm. One bigger, more dangerous claw grew out of each leg.

When a raptor pounced,
it used these horrible claws
to slash at its prey.

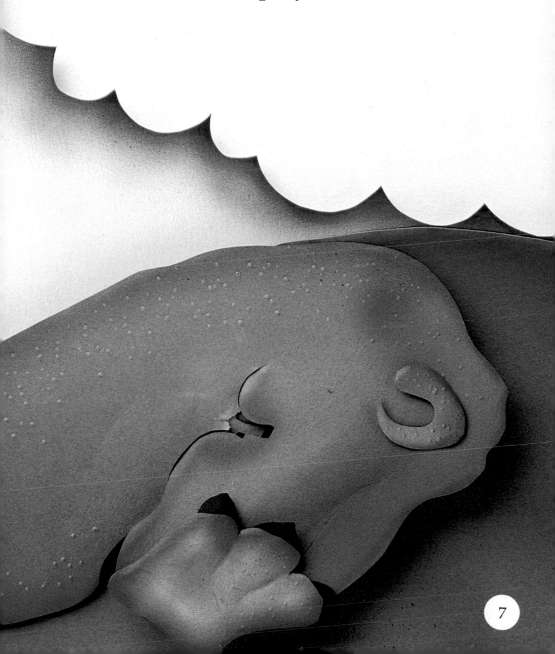

Raptors were among
the smallest dinosaurs
ever to have lived. Some raptors stood
only six feet tall. That's about as tall
as a grown man. Imagine how tiny
these raptors looked next to the huge
Tyrannosaurus!

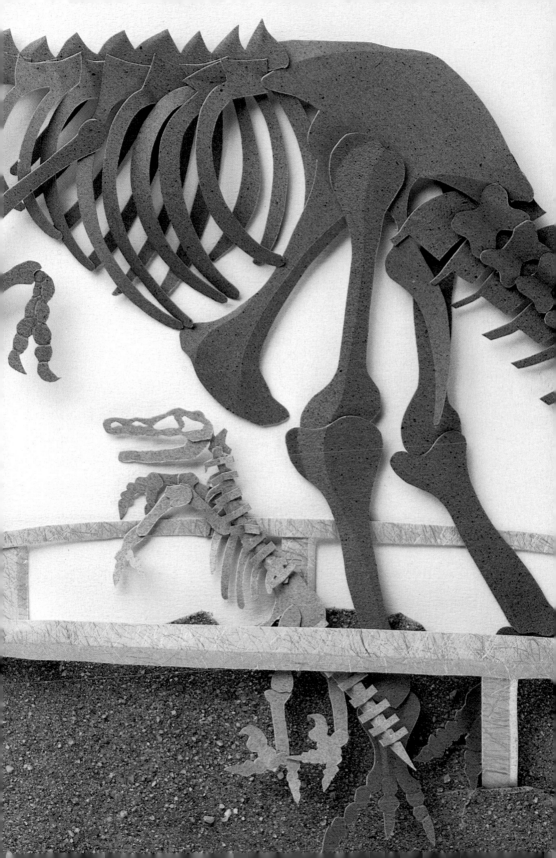

Even though they were
small, raptors were deadly
hunters. Raptors' eyes
pointed forward on their
faces, just like your eyes do.
Their special eyes helped
raptors see how far away
their prey was.

Raptors were fast, too!
They would chase small
animals and grab them
with their long fingers.

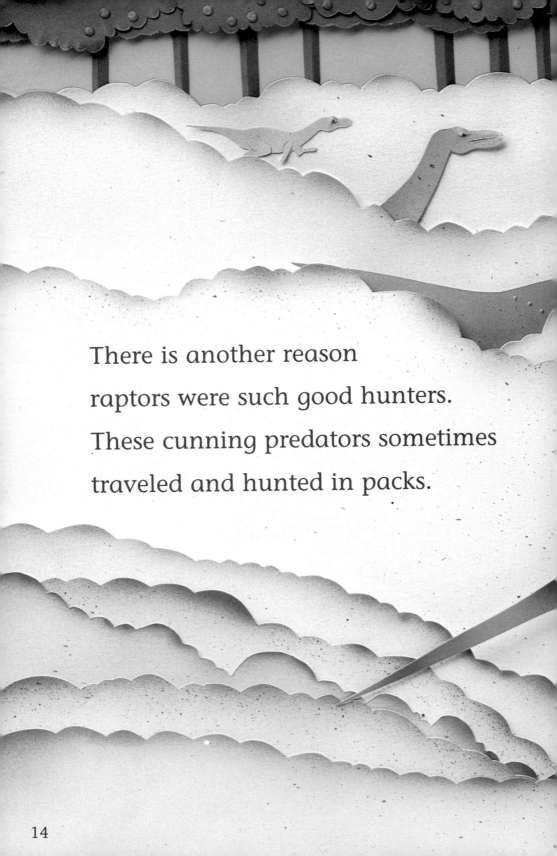

There is another reason
raptors were such good hunters.
These cunning predators sometimes
traveled and hunted in packs.

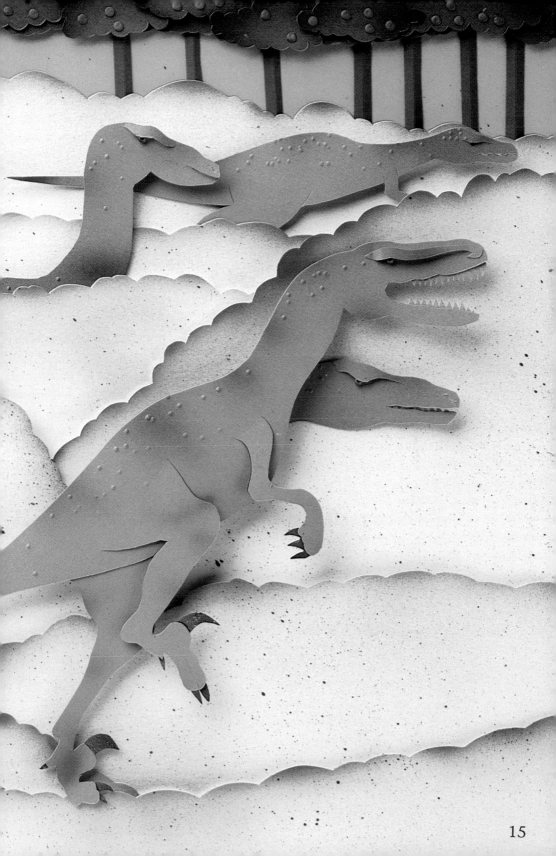

When they
spotted a victim,
they would attack as
a group. This way,
raptors could kill dinosaurs
much bigger than they were.

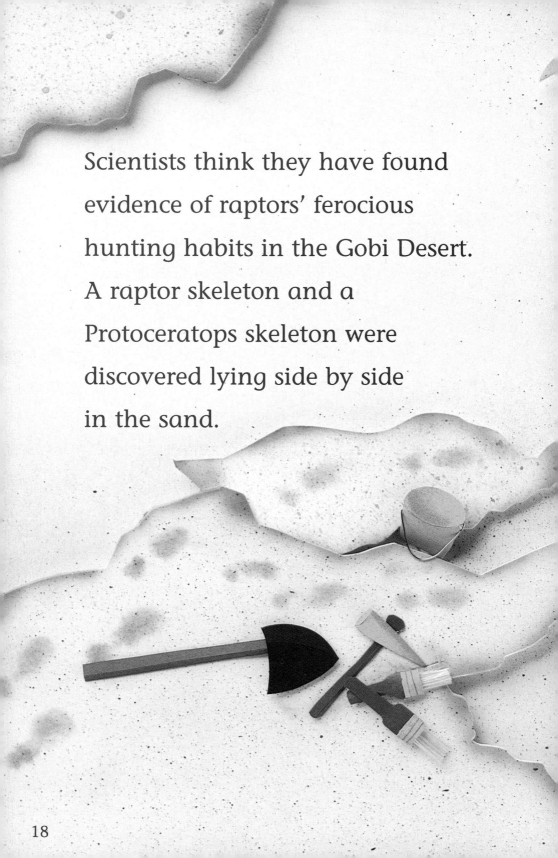

Scientists think they have found
evidence of raptors' ferocious
hunting habits in the Gobi Desert.
A raptor skeleton and a
Protoceratops skeleton were
discovered lying side by side
in the sand.

How did these two dinosaurs end up like this? Perhaps a group of raptors attacked the Protoceratops. As it fought back, the Protoceratops clamped its jaws down on one raptor's arm and held on.

The other raptors
probably killed and ate
the Protoceratops and
went on their way.
The unlucky raptor
was left behind.

No one really knows what
color raptors, or any dinosaurs,
were. Many scientists think they
may have been as colorful as
snakes, lizards, and birds are today.

The dinosaurs' skin colors and patterns probably blended in with their surroundings. This allowed them to hide from enemies. These colors and patterns may also have helped the dinosaurs attract mates.

Some scientists think raptors might even have had feathers. What do you think raptors looked like?

Raptors lived in the late Cretaceous period (66 million years ago), which means that they were one of the very last kinds of dinosaurs to become extinct.

What happened to all the dinosaurs?
Did they all get sick and never
get well?

Did a huge chunk of space rock crash into Earth, killing the plants and animals that dinosaurs ate?

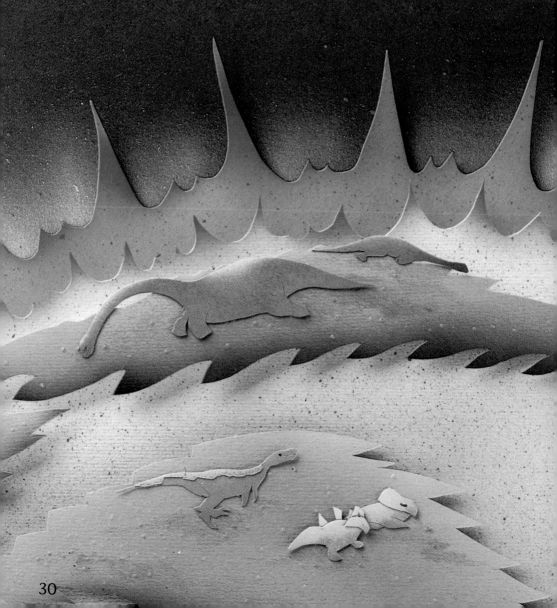

We may never know for sure. But what we do know is that the raptor was one of the fiercest, most terrifying dinosaurs of all.

Index